Smoky Joe's book of Drawing Ponies

Smoky Joe's book of Drawing Ponies

Top tips, techniques and pony stuff – straight from the horse's mouth!

with Jennifer Bell

J.A. ALLEN · LONDON

ISBN 978 0 85131 978 0

J.A. Allen
Clerkenwell House
Clerkenwell Green
London EC1R OHT

J.A. Allen is an imprint of Robert Hale Limited

www.allenbooks.co.uk

A catalogue record for this book is available from the British Library

Conceived and illustrated by Jennifer Bell
Design by Paul Saunders
Edited by Martin Diggle

Printed by Midas Printing International Limited, China

ACKNOWLEDGEMENT

My thanks to Sandy Anderson at Thistledown Stud,
and Dani, Rebecca, and Georgina.

Contents

About this Book 6–7

Games with Shapes 8–9

Every Pony Is Different 10

Meet Us! – Trevor, Rosie and Smoky Joe (ME!) 11–13

Time to get X-ray Vision 14–15

Perspective 16–17

Getting the Details Right 18–21

Black and White Drawing 22–23

Felt Tips 24–25

Crayons 26–27

Pastels 28–29

Pen and Ink 30–31

Backgrounds 32–33

Drawing from Life 34–35

Pony Portraits 36–37

Accessories 38–39

Riders 40–41

Fantasy 42–43

Humour 44–45

Ponies from the Past 46–47

Info plus 48

About this Book

Hmmm...

Brilliant idea coming up.

I've noticed that there are lots of great books by artists who like drawing horses...

But then I thought... what would be nicer (and more useful) than a book on... DRAWING REAL PONIES? ... and it could be from MY point of view!!! So...this is it!

He's up to something.

Smoky Joe's Book of Drawing Ponies

Featuring ME, TREVOR and ROSIE (but mostly me...).

This is us boys: large as life and twice as daft – going head to head to see who cracks first... then shake it all about... and...

and...

and...

So read on! Get your sketchbook and pencils, and by the end of the book you'll be thinking of yourself as an equestrian **ARTIST!**

And you can keep in touch, too! We've got a website: www.drawingponies.com

GO! GO! GO!

While Rosie talks to the pretty flowers...

Hello, pretty flowers...

You shouldn't try to make friends with your food.

It'll end in tears...

Games with Shapes

These are the shapes you need to build up into a pony.

Just circles and lines to start with...

Me, straight from the field, and posing prettily!'

A tracing will give you an accurate outline, which is useful sometimes.

But it's also confusing! (Which leg is in front?) It gives you no **REAL** information about the pony.

Outline

BUT

If you can see how the circles and lines are put together to make this shape (me just standing), you'll start to **understand** its **structure**...and **understanding structure** will make your drawings convincing!

Seeing the basic shapes

These basic shapes will help you to draw ponies in action, as well as getting the proportions right!

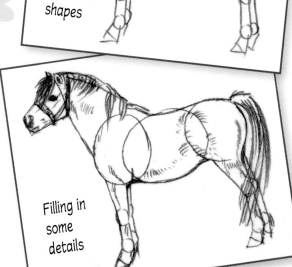

Filling in some details

Building Up

An egg?

Set the pony's ears in the gap between the head and neck wedges.

Set his neck into his chest.

Some rough guidelines (not rules!) for proportions:
Depth of tum = length of leg = length of neck
Knees are about halfway down the leg; hocks are a little bit higher

When you've got the hang of using circles and lines to draw ponies from the side (two dimensions), start to think in three dimensions – the circles become spheres, the lines become cones and cylinders...and you can build up a pony shape from any angle – it's just like geometry...clever stuff!

I am going to hatch this if it's the last thing I do

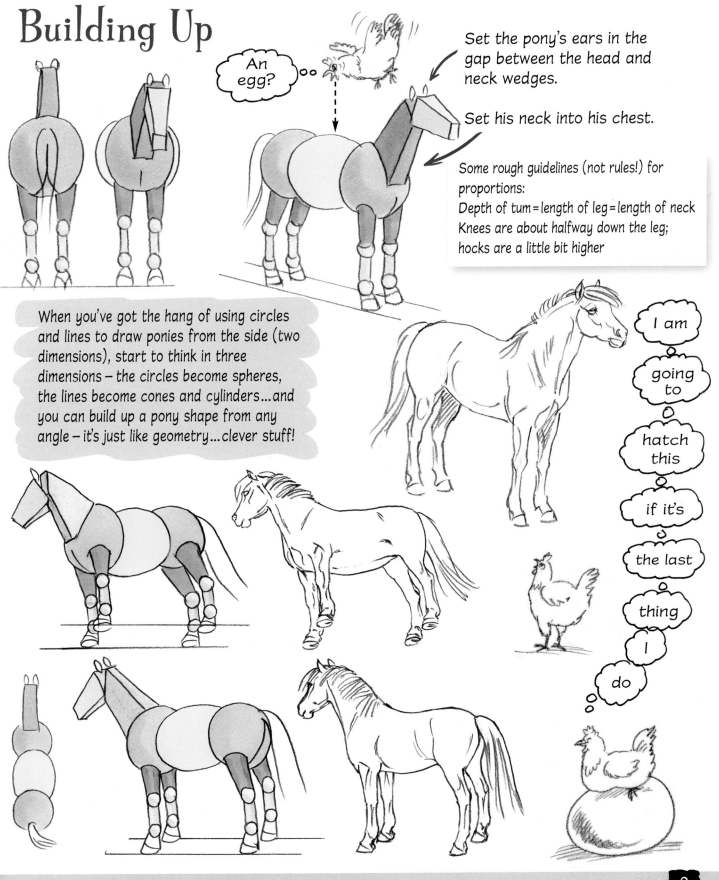

Every Pony is Different

...and we are typical of the three pony shapes.

Smoky Joe...

Rosie

Trevor

...ME!

...ME!

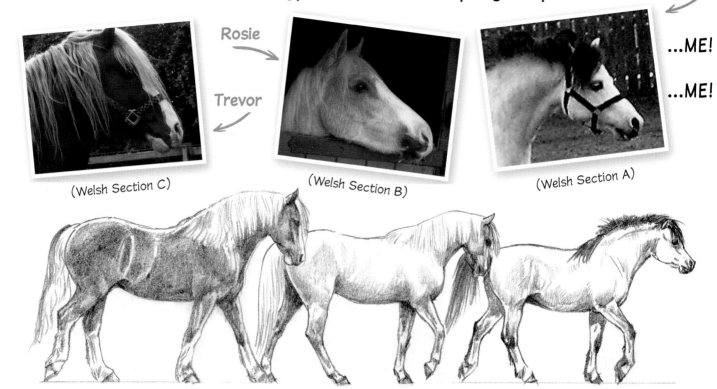

(Welsh Section C)

(Welsh Section B)

(Welsh Section A)

We ponies aren't always beautiful and elegant and romantic*...we've got **PERSONALITY AND ATTITUDE** – we can be cheeky and playful and friendly and moody and dynamic and sleepy and... and...and...and when you draw us, you're learning so much more than just how to create shapes – you're learning about **PONY LIFE!**

*well, Rosie is...

If you can draw us, you can draw any pony!

SO HERE'S HOW TO DRAW
Real Ponies (US!)

To introduce us – here's me pretending to be a bucking bronco – I can see Rosie and Trevor are obviously impressed!

Meet Us... Trevor ★

Lovely wavy hairdo with two tones and highlights!

Trevor's a real chum — handsome, strong and chunky. And he's light on his feet for a big pony!

He's got great curves (well, he's almost circular from behind). When he rolls it looks as if he's got a huge tum; actually it's not bigger than usual...but his ribcage is pushed up...

...and his shoulders and hips have folded down.

He must have heard the breakfast bucket calling him!!!

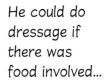

He could do dressage if there was food involved...

Mane and tail and fetlock feathers flying in the breeze...

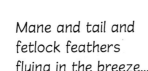
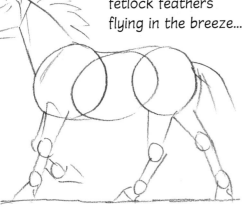

He's like a steam train when he gets going!

Hello fairies. ₒₒₒ

She's often in a world of her own! Pony fairies?...Oh really!

Rosie

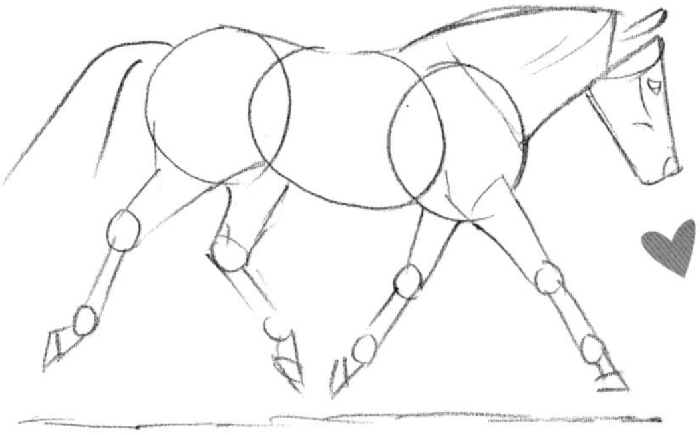

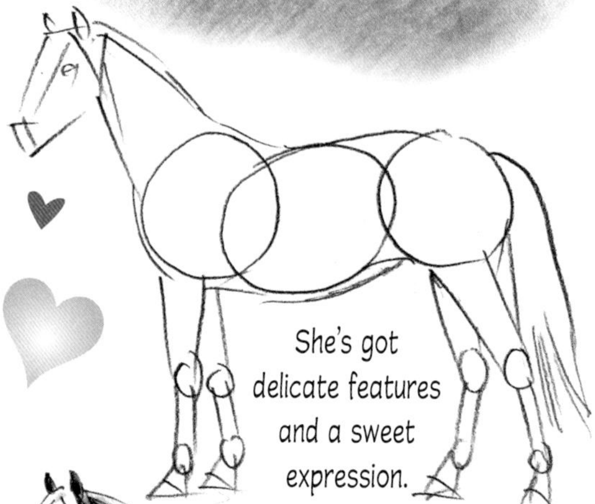

Pretty
pink pony
Twinkletoes
My pal
Rosie!

Dancing on air

?? Hmmm... anything's possible... ₒₒₒ

She's got delicate features and a sweet expression.

All glammed up for winning prizes.

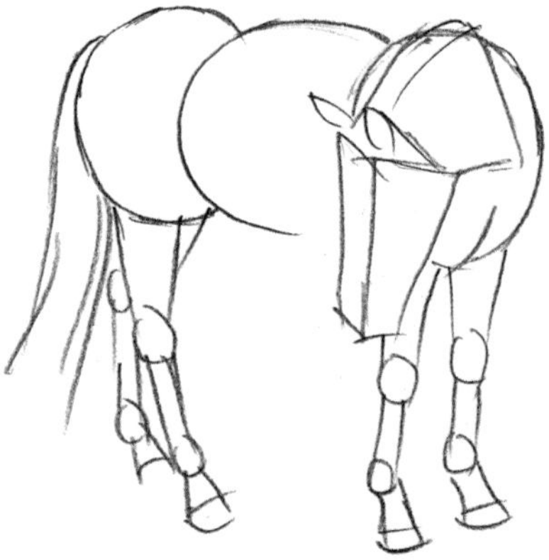

Rosie's world must be...

...strange but wonderful!

Me

BOSS PONY

Smoky Joe

ME ★ ME ★

THE INFINITE VARIETY OF **ME!**

Yeah, yeah

Just day-dreaming

Romantic hero... cheeky chappie... I can do it all!

Smoky Joe, the circus pony

Got things to do...get to places...and fast...and...nobody – but nobody – gets in my way!

If you know how it works, YOU CAN DRAW IT! SO –

Time to get X-Ray Vision

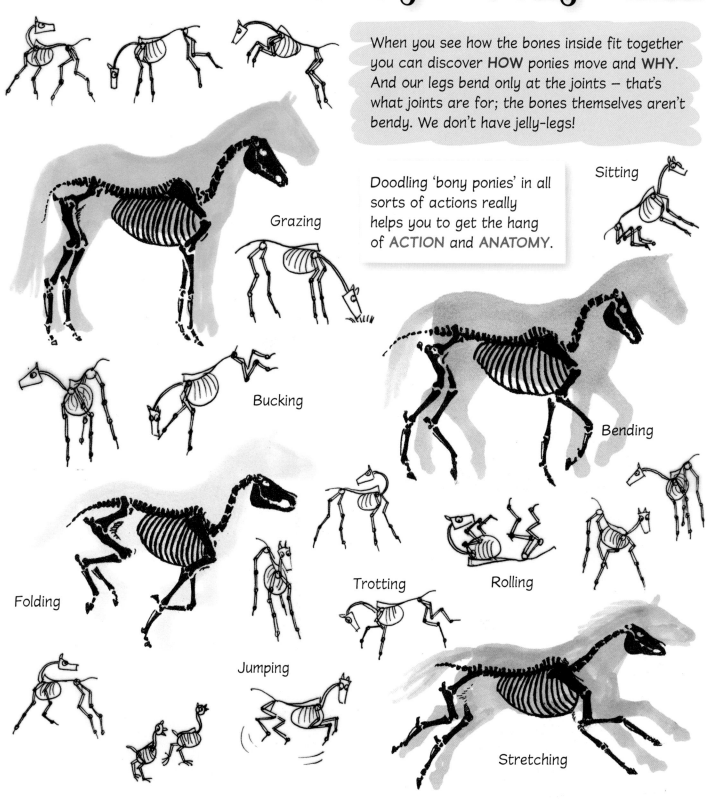

When you see how the bones inside fit together you can discover **HOW** ponies move and **WHY**. And our legs bend only at the joints – that's what joints are for; the bones themselves aren't bendy. We don't have jelly-legs!

Doodling 'bony ponies' in all sorts of actions really helps you to get the hang of **ACTION** and **ANATOMY**.

Sitting

Grazing

Bucking

Bending

Folding

Trotting

Rolling

Jumping

Stretching

How Do the Bones Work?

(Hint – the brain talks to the muscles attached to the bones)

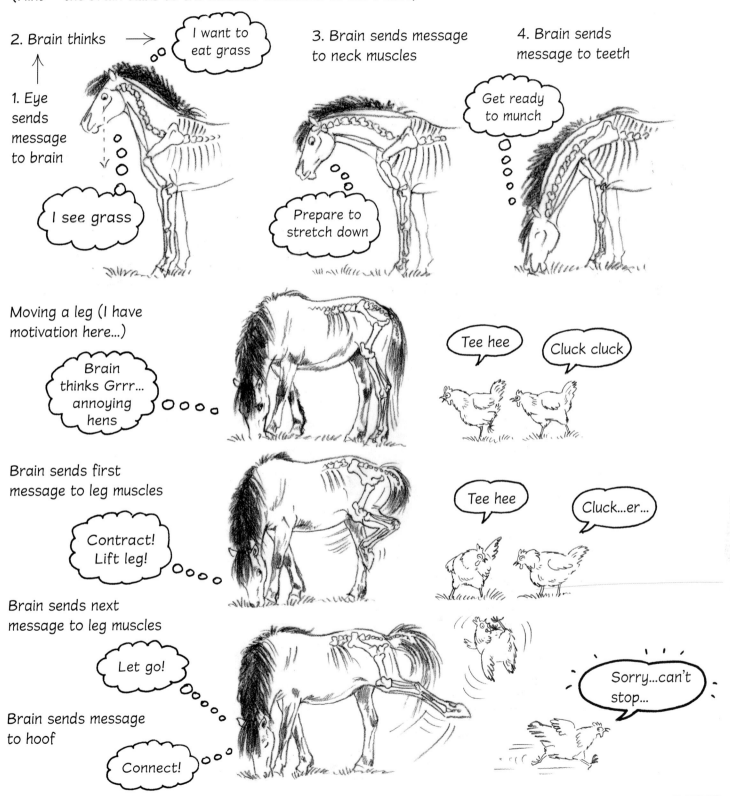

2. Brain thinks → I want to eat grass

1. Eye sends message to brain

I see grass

3. Brain sends message to neck muscles

Prepare to stretch down

4. Brain sends message to teeth

Get ready to munch

Moving a leg (I have motivation here...)

Brain thinks Grrr... annoying hens

Tee hee

Cluck cluck

Brain sends first message to leg muscles

Contract! Lift leg!

Tee hee

Cluck...er...

Brain sends next message to leg muscles

Let go!

Brain sends message to hoof

Connect!

Sorry...can't stop...

Perspective

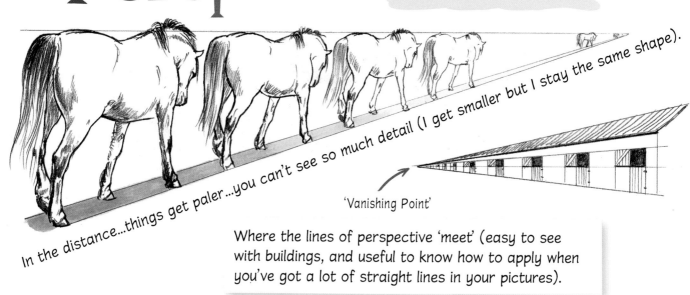

In the distance...things get paler...you can't see so much detail (I get smaller but I stay the same shape).

'Vanishing Point'

Where the lines of perspective 'meet' (easy to see with buildings, and useful to know how to apply when you've got a lot of straight lines in your pictures).

In **THE FOREGROUND** spend more time on the details close to you – use stronger colours and stronger lines.

In **THE BACKGROUND** use paler colours to create a sense of depth.

Will Trevor get to the bucket first? Or will Trevor (or Trevor) beat him to it?

Foreshortening (PERSPECTIVE UP **CLOSE**)

Side view

You see one eye, an ear, all of one cheek.

Three-quarter view

Turning... foreshortening...

If I turn to face you, my head is foreshortened.

Two eyes, two ears, all of the muzzle, but only part of two cheeks and they're at an angle...

THINK BACK TO THE BASIC SHAPES
Imagine them turning, and you can see them from lots of angles.

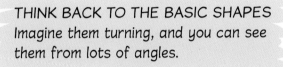

If I see you creeping up behind me...

 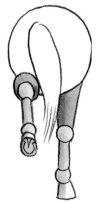 

...I may be tempted to kick (I mean foreshorten) you...

I could try to show you foreshortening of all four legs at once but...

...I'd fall over.

Getting the Details Right

THE EARS sit either side and behind the top bony bit

Skeleton

Jaw bone

Socket for the eyeball, which is held in by the eye muscles

Nostril tubes go up here

Muscles

Ear muscles

Neck muscles

Eye muscles

Mouth muscles

YELLOW for the bony bits that show through the skin

PINK for the muscles you need to remember

Shorthand sketch marks

Use these as 'landmarks', when you sketch – they'll help you to get your drawings accurate and looking real.

More finished drawing

You too can have ears like mine! You just need thick felt and some Plasticine (stick them onto a plastic Alice band).

The ears have a language all of their own

Oooh! Hello!

Er...do I know you?

Go away!

Top eye muscles in action

Mine

Yours

The ears can also say...

Breakfast?

Breakfast, but I don't want to be caught...

I'm pretending to be asleep...

I've bumped against an electric fence!

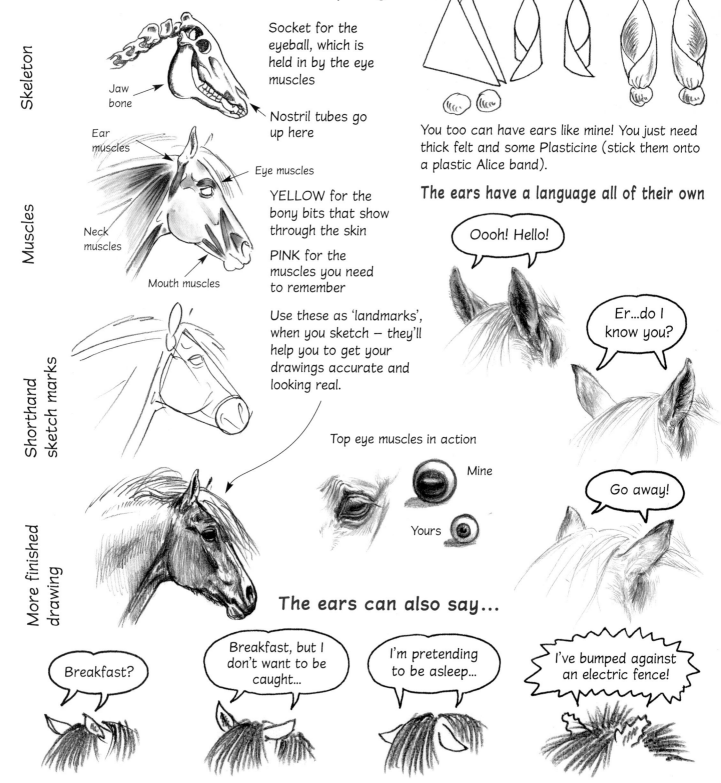

18

More Interesting Bits

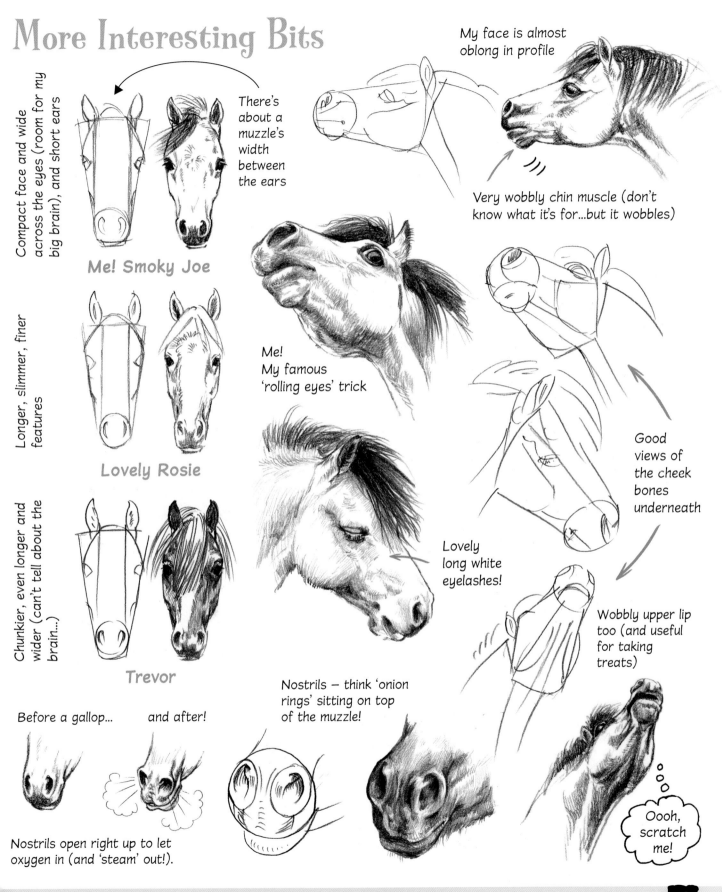

There's about a muzzle's width between the ears

Compact face and wide across the eyes (room for my big brain), and short ears

Me! Smoky Joe

Longer, slimmer, finer features

Lovely Rosie

Chunkier, even longer and wider (can't tell about the brain...)

Trevor

Before a gallop...   and after!

Nostrils open right up to let oxygen in (and 'steam' out!).

Me! My famous 'rolling eyes' trick

Lovely long white eyelashes!

Nostrils – think 'onion rings' sitting on top of the muzzle!

My face is almost oblong in profile

Very wobbly chin muscle (don't know what it's for...but it wobbles)

Good views of the cheek bones underneath

Wobbly upper lip too (and useful for taking treats)

Oooh, scratch me!

Manes and Tails and...

Hairy bits are lovely to draw — there are so many different styles, and they can really illustrate a pony's personality!

Mine; wiry and generously hairy (well, it *is* if you look on the other side) with a certain untameable character...

Soft, silky and straight mane and tail — Rosie's got her own hairdresser who pulls it to keep it neat and nice.

Trevor tossing his amazing locks.

A huge variety of lovely colours in Trevor's flaxen mane and tail.

Me, looking my best for the camera.

Someone...hem... suggested to Trevor that he put his best foot forward...

Pretty toes – not hairy at all

Slightly hairy heels

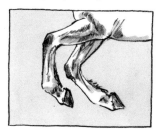

Fully feathered

...Hoofy, Jointy Bits

Keep in mind the basic shapes that make up the legs — remember the bones...

...Then think about the muscles and ligaments that you can see under the skin.

Make a working model of the legs with card and paperclips!

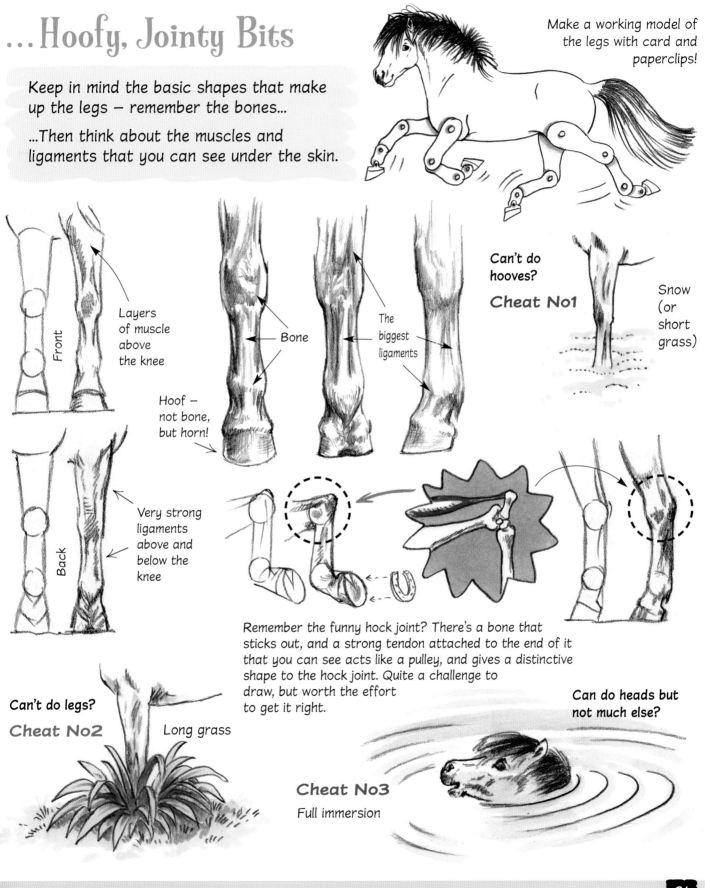

Front

Layers of muscle above the knee

Bone

The biggest ligaments

Hoof — not bone, but horn!

Can't do hooves?

Cheat No1

Snow (or short grass)

Back

Very strong ligaments above and below the knee

Remember the funny hock joint? There's a bone that sticks out, and a strong tendon attached to the end of it that you can see acts like a pulley, and gives a distinctive shape to the hock joint. Quite a challenge to draw, but worth the effort to get it right.

Can't do legs?

Cheat No2

Long grass

Can do heads but not much else?

Cheat No3

Full immersion

21

Black and White Drawing

Conté crayons and sticks – like pencils but waxier and in browns (and other colours) as well as black.

Hard charcoal pencil

Chalk and soft charcoal

Soft pencils (2B, 4B, etc.)

Hard pencils (H, HB, etc.)

4B

2B

HB

Try out lots of different techniques – especially the messy ones! Don't be anxious about finishing everything off beautifully; ALL your drawings (even the finished ones) are just preparation for the next. You will get better and better *if you practise.*

SAMPLE

4B pencil on sm-o-o-oth paper; it's black where the pencil's pressed hard, and grey where it's pressed more lightly.

SAMPLE

4B pencil on thick cartridge paper (it's produced a rougher line; wouldn't be so good for fine drawing).

SAMPLE

HB pencil on smooth paper; fine, light pencil strokes for lots of detail.

PAPER

Smooth paper (layout or printer paper, some sketch pads).

Thick cartridge (a rougher surface).

Watercolour paper (deeper indentations)...and pastel paper can be even rougher.

SAMPLE

Charcoal pencil – it can be sharpened (carefully though) so you can draw detail.

Smudging is effective...in the right places...

...BUT DIRTY MARKS AREN'T!

Charcoal creates a lot of black dust so...

TIP – work on a board or a pad that you can keep upright.

TIP – keep washing your hands.

TIP – spray with a fixative afterwards.

Soft charcoal is great for BIG DRAWINGS where you need lots of black...

Have you got a wall to spare?

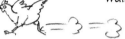

SAMPLE

Just chalk (with a bit of charcoal detail on the top) on black paper.

SAMPLE

Conté crayons in several shades of brown (with a bit of white chalk) on grey paper.

Felt Tips

Professional spirit markers are double-ended (thick and thin) and are blendable – add another colour layer before the first one dries. Yes, they're more expensive, but you can buy them individually in subtle colours as well as in sets. And they *last* much longer.

Get the best you can – cheap felt tips don't have much ink in – frustrating!

Thin felt tips are best for just drawing with (not colouring in). Try hatching and cross-hatching to build up a shape.

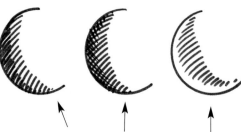

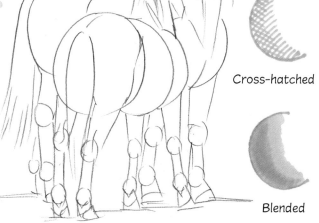

Cross-hatched

Blended

Hatching and cross-hatching showing the curve of a shape with a shadow.

Hatching that shows the curve *without* a shadow.

This picture is built up with these colours.

SAMPLES
Started off with broad strokes of the pale colours, and overlaid with progressively stronger colours that blend. Detail is added carefully with dark colour at the end.

TIP You don't have to colour in the whole pony. Just a few curved lines can show 'roundness' – you can leave lots of white for contrast.

Dark colours can indicate shading and shadows.

Same colours – orange and brown – but different effects.

Or use dots?

A swarm of midges

An appaloosa in a swarm of midges

Sometimes very simple colour drawings are really effective...sketch in pencil, go over the lines with felt tips then rub out the pencil.

TIP Drawing quickly can give you **CONFIDENCE!**

Crayons

THEY DON'T STAIN, SPILL OR LEAK!

Lots of really easy to use colours, but don't use just one colour – get subtle effects by overlaying several colours (start with the palest colour).

For pale colours just press lightly

Pale and interesting

Bright and beautiful

Press harder for brighter colours

Pencil crayons (used dry) work best on *smooth* paper, and the colours will be more intense than if used on cartridge or rough paper.

Pink, orange and dark brown

Orange, rust brown, dark brown and black

Blue, lavender, grey and black

Water-soluble Crayons

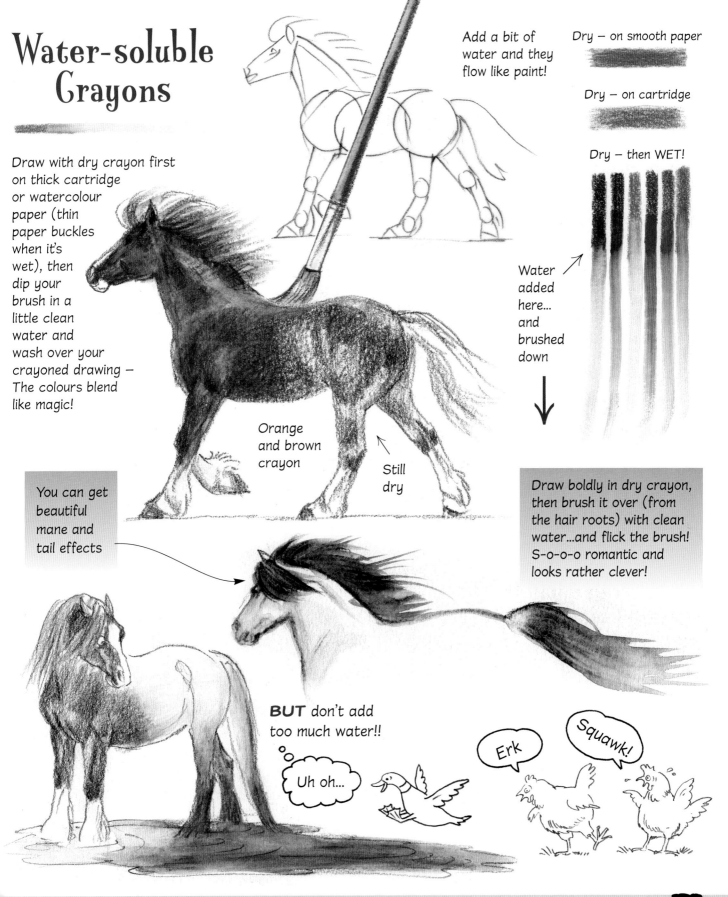

Draw with dry crayon first on thick cartridge or watercolour paper (thin paper buckles when it's wet), then dip your brush in a little clean water and wash over your crayoned drawing – The colours blend like magic!

Add a bit of water and they flow like paint!

Dry – on smooth paper

Dry – on cartridge

Dry – then WET!

Water added here... and brushed down

Orange and brown crayon

Still dry

You can get beautiful mane and tail effects

Draw boldly in dry crayon, then brush it over (from the hair roots) with clean water...and flick the brush! S-o-o-o romantic and looks rather clever!

BUT don't add too much water!!

Uh oh...

Erk

Squawk!

Pastels

Oil Pastels

Bright, strong colours in inexpensive sets...but you can also buy subtle and beautiful colours individually.

Oil pastels are great for impressionistic effects with thick stripes and dots of colour.

You can sharpen them if you need to with an ordinary kitchen knife.

Lay down the pale colours first and build up to strong and dark colours. (Be careful you don't pick up *more* colour than you put down!)

AND you can get

Delicate effects too!

Rosie's covered all over with pale pink crayon, with a bit of red and dark brown...

OR – experiment with blending them with a bit of turps or white spirit on a brush – Very nearly oil painting!

then tiny lines are scraped through to the white paper with a cocktail stick (cross-hatching creating highlights, not shadows.)

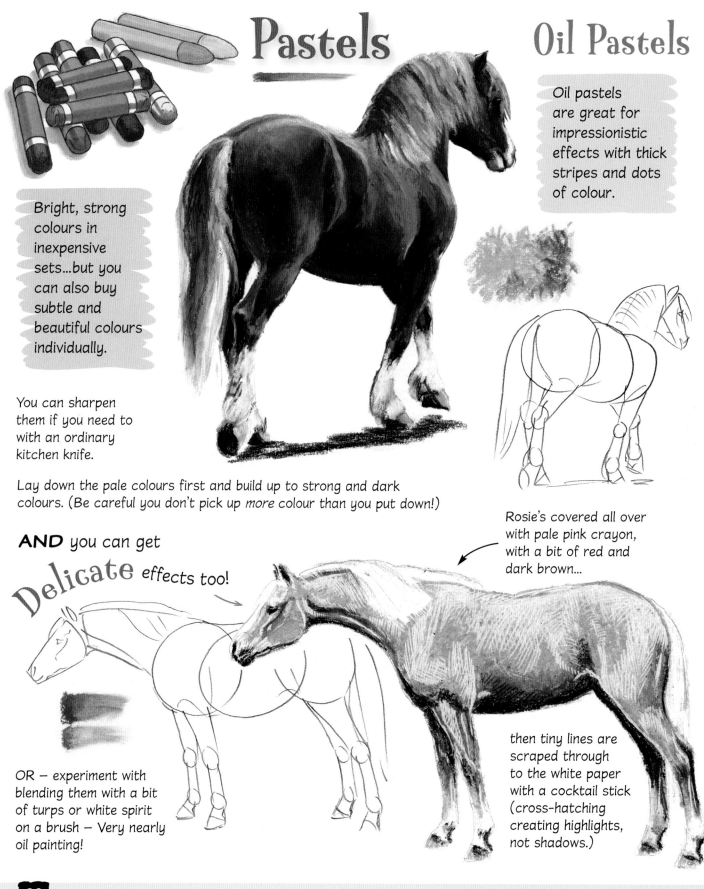

Soft Pastels

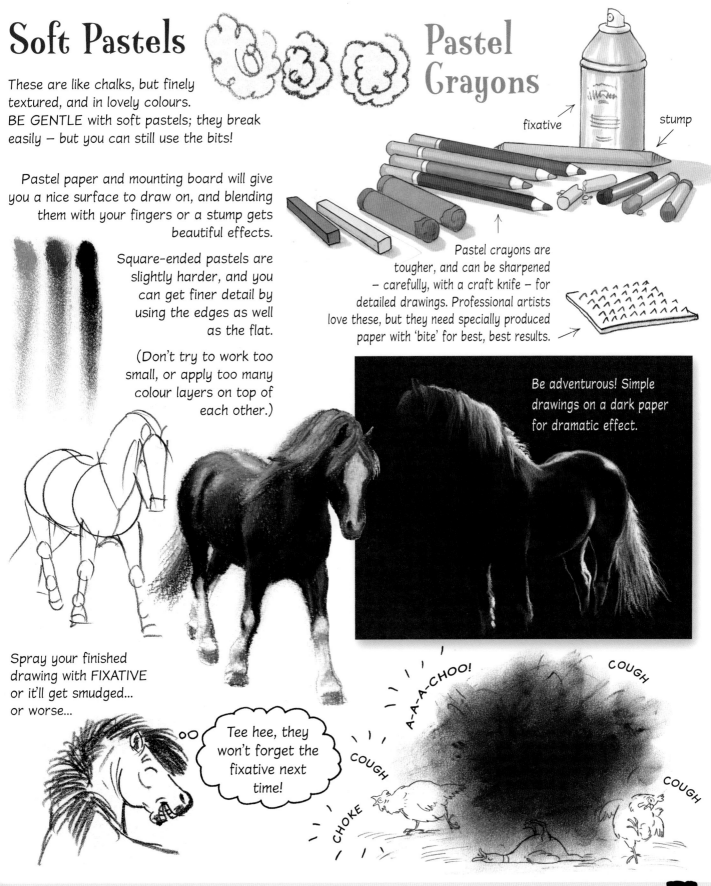

These are like chalks, but finely textured, and in lovely colours. BE GENTLE with soft pastels; they break easily – but you can still use the bits!

Pastel paper and mounting board will give you a nice surface to draw on, and blending them with your fingers or a stump gets beautiful effects.

Square-ended pastels are slightly harder, and you can get finer detail by using the edges as well as the flat.

(Don't try to work too small, or apply too many colour layers on top of each other.)

Spray your finished drawing with FIXATIVE or it'll get smudged... or worse...

Pastel Crayons

fixative

stump

Pastel crayons are tougher, and can be sharpened – carefully, with a craft knife – for detailed drawings. Professional artists love these, but they need specially produced paper with 'bite' for best, best results.

Be adventurous! Simple drawings on a dark paper for dramatic effect.

Tee hee, they won't forget the fixative next time!

A-A-A-CHOO!

COUGH

COUGH

COUGH

CHOKE

29

Pen and Ink

Use your pen like a pencil – the technique is the same – be confident and work freely... slow lines are wobbly lines...

Doodling

A famous artist once said: 'Drawing is like taking a line for a walk.'

Some walks are fun and others should be more disciplined – some lines need a bit of training!

to DESIGN

...ink DOES need a bit of boldness...you can't rub it out!

Every line can make a statement! Every line matters!

Just the necessary

Cross-hatching to the X-treme!

...Whether it's drawing the **BARE MINIMUM** ink over your pencil sketch, then rubbing out the pencil lines (wait till the ink's dry!!)...

...Or the **ABSOLUTE MAXIMUM**...just keep going! Use fine but deliberate lines that build up a solid and convincing shape.

Make the shadows work for you. You **DON'T HAVE TO DRAW EVERYTHING!**

Shadows make good drawings **GREAT.**

Look at pictures of ponies in the sun...experiment with model ponies and a torch!

Be **VERY BOLD** with just black and white. It looks bleached out. Don't even think about the grey areas!!

Just the **SHINY HIGHLIGHTS**

No more Rosie the Pink Pony...I'm the Dark Lady now...

Cluck CLUCK cluck cluck C...L...U...C...K!

Gloss paint huh?

Oh, right...enough in there to paint another pony so I'd better be polite...

Backgrounds

Sooner or later you're going to want to see your ponies in a **SETTING** so think **WHY** they are there and **WHAT YOU WANT TO SAY.**

1. Create a SENSE OF PLACE.

You don't have to spend hours on the background – sometimes a few lines are enough to say where you are!

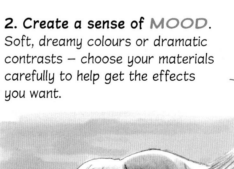

2. Create a sense of MOOD.

Soft, dreamy colours or dramatic contrasts – choose your materials carefully to help get the effects you want.

3. Create a sense of STORYTELLING

Make people *take more than one look* at your picture...
Make them interested in what's going on...tell a story.

Ask questions of your picture:
Is there:
...a relationship?
...a dialogue?
...a before and an after?

Your imagination can invent whole worlds you can explore in your drawings –
You can make the impossible **REAL!**

Same drawing of me, but in different stories!

...But I know which story I'd choose here...

YOU'RE THE ARTIST –
You can choose the stories you want to tell.

Drawing from Life

If you can draw a passable pony from memory, you have the skills to try drawing from life as well!

Before photography, this is how artists learnt their stuff! So...you've got a sketchbook and a pony to draw – just have a go.

STEP 1
What do you see? Thinks... rough overall shape.

STEP 2
Thinks...How do the basic shapes fit into that?

STEP 3
Thinks...What's special about this pony? Make lots of observations, e.g. 'nice top line'.

A distinct triangle for his withers.

His shoulders slope at this angle.

There's a really round rump! Good view of hock.

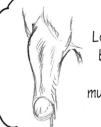 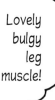
Lovely bulgy leg muscle!

He's got a lovely long tail, slightly wavy, dark in the centre.

A long, soft mane, draped like curtains.

A strange view of his head! Jaws are an interesting shape, and the headcollar divides up the view.

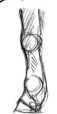
He's got a knobbly knee seen from the back.

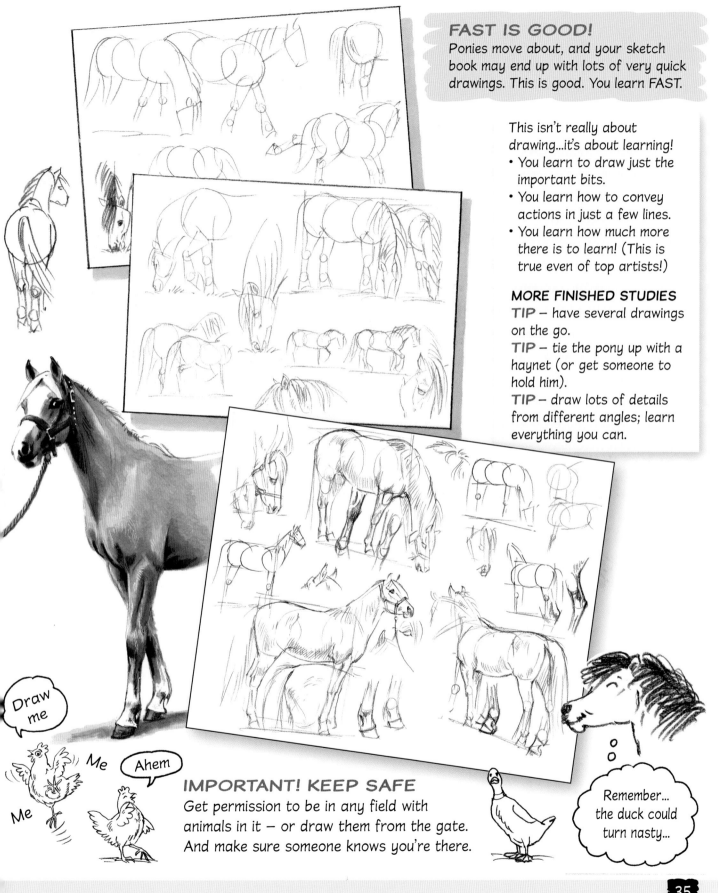

FAST IS GOOD!
Ponies move about, and your sketch book may end up with lots of very quick drawings. This is good. You learn FAST.

This isn't really about drawing...it's about learning!
- You learn to draw just the important bits.
- You learn how to convey actions in just a few lines.
- You learn how much more there is to learn! (This is true even of top artists!)

MORE FINISHED STUDIES
TIP – have several drawings on the go.

TIP – tie the pony up with a haynet (or get someone to hold him).

TIP – draw lots of details from different angles; learn everything you can.

Draw me

Me

Ahem

Me

IMPORTANT! KEEP SAFE
Get permission to be in any field with animals in it – or draw them from the gate. And make sure someone knows you're there.

Remember... the duck could turn nasty...

Pony Portraits

It's easiest to work from a good reference photo BUT which photo would you choose?

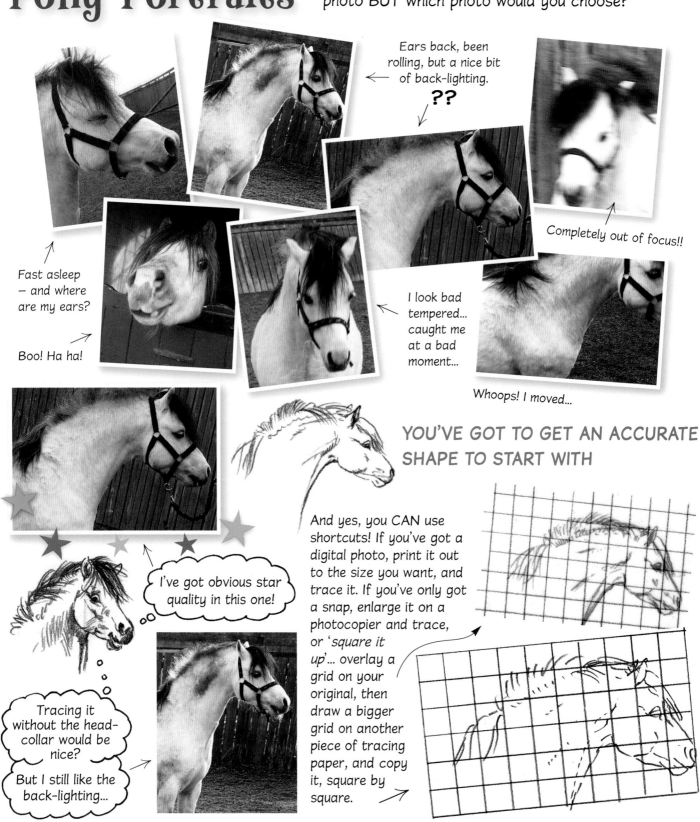

Ears back, been rolling, but a nice bit of back-lighting.

??

Completely out of focus!!

Fast asleep – and where are my ears?

Boo! Ha ha!

I look bad tempered... caught me at a bad moment...

Whoops! I moved...

YOU'VE GOT TO GET AN ACCURATE SHAPE TO START WITH

I've got obvious star quality in this one!

Tracing it without the head-collar would be nice?

But I still like the back-lighting...

And yes, you CAN use shortcuts! If you've got a digital photo, print it out to the size you want, and trace it. If you've only got a snap, enlarge it on a photocopier and trace, or 'square it up'... overlay a grid on your original, then draw a bigger grid on another piece of tracing paper, and copy it, square by square.

How to transfer a trace

Blacken the **reverse** of your trace (using the side of a pencil), tape the trace to your paper and go over the outline again (ballpoint is good) and a dark line gets transferred.

It's really important to have a good photo to work from – one that shows lots of detail – and is in focus! Keep looking at your photo as you draw, thinking: how can I portray textures, depth and personality as well as getting the shape right?

Think about doing the background (if you want one) before you *completely* finish the portrait itself – it'll allow you to touch up your drawing with a flourish!

BACKGROUNDS: what do you like drawing – landscapes? Skies? Fantasy? Patterns? Does your portrait just need a plain background – or a cloudy mixture? Complementing or contrasting?

You get
HAPPY PICTURES
when the sun shines!

Highlight and shadows make your drawing look extra-real.

TIP – if you want to draw onto coloured or dark paper, spread chalk or pastel onto the reverse of your trace – and then press the outline through with a ballpoint.

A dark background shows up that nice bit of back-lighting.

A dull day...

Hey! The sun's out!

Accessories

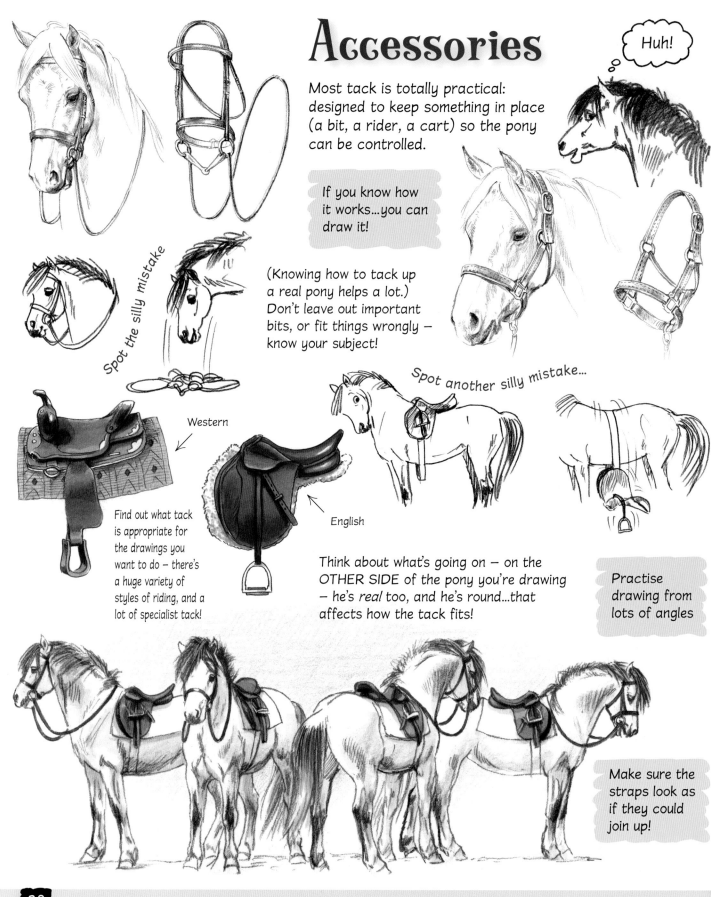

Huh!

Most tack is totally practical: designed to keep something in place (a bit, a rider, a cart) so the pony can be controlled.

If you know how it works...you can draw it!

(Knowing how to tack up a real pony helps a lot.) Don't leave out important bits, or fit things wrongly – know your subject!

Spot the silly mistake

Spot another silly mistake...

Western

English

Find out what tack is appropriate for the drawings you want to do – there's a huge variety of styles of riding, and a lot of specialist tack!

Think about what's going on – on the OTHER SIDE of the pony you're drawing – he's *real* too, and he's round...that affects how the tack fits!

Practise drawing from lots of angles

Make sure the straps look as if they could join up!

More accessories

Riders

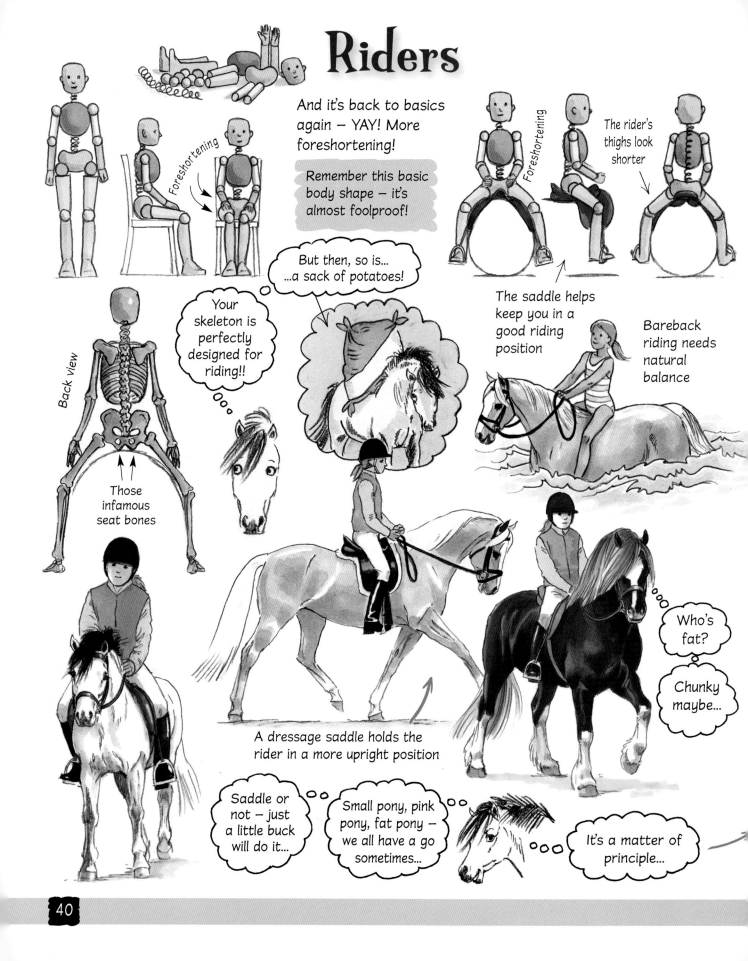

And it's back to basics again – YAY! More foreshortening!

Remember this basic body shape – it's almost foolproof!

Foreshortening

Foreshortening

The rider's thighs look shorter

But then, so is...
...a sack of potatoes!

Your skeleton is perfectly designed for riding!!

Back view

Those infamous seat bones

The saddle helps keep you in a good riding position

Bareback riding needs natural balance

A dressage saddle holds the rider in a more upright position

Who's fat?

Chunky maybe...

Saddle or not – just a little buck will do it...

Small pony, pink pony, fat pony – we all have a go sometimes...

It's a matter of principle...

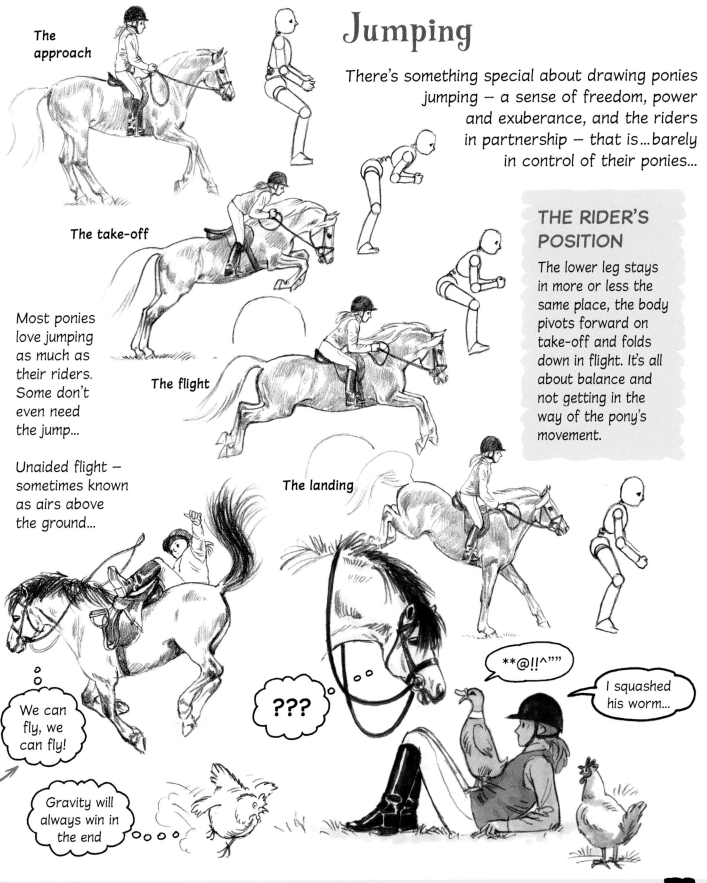

Jumping

There's something special about drawing ponies jumping – a sense of freedom, power and exuberance, and the riders in partnership – that is...barely in control of their ponies...

The approach

The take-off

Most ponies love jumping as much as their riders. Some don't even need the jump...

The flight

Unaided flight – sometimes known as airs above the ground...

The landing

THE RIDER'S POSITION

The lower leg stays in more or less the same place, the body pivots forward on take-off and folds down in flight. It's all about balance and not getting in the way of the pony's movement.

Could it be real?
Fantasy

How far can your imagination take you?

??

Could ponies fly? Really?
How would it all work? Would the wings be like arms – extending from the shoulder? How big would they need to be? This big? Bigger?

Photos of real owl's wings used as references.

Borrowing fashion styles from Renaissance Italy gives a fairytale illustration a sense of **strange reality.**

TIP 1
A bit of real-life detail in your fantasy will help make the whole picture convincing.

TIP 2
Your fantasy world needs
INTERNAL LOGIC
Get curious about how
the **IMPOSSIBLE.**
could be made
POSSIBLE!

TIP 3
Tell a good story in your
picture – something has
just happened...something
is about to happen...

That's my boy!

Misty, magical and romantic – lots is left to the imagination. (Well, we don't know a lot about unicorns...)

??
The centaur's spine must be an extension of his equine backbone... but does he have two hearts? Two pairs of lungs? Would this give him extraordinary powers?

The pony's found his true vocation!

...And then, back to REAL LIFE...

The first duty of a pony is to spread a little...mud...

Humour

How to start

1. Trace a nice picture

Expressions, situations, surprises, consequences, relationships, reactions, *everything* has its funny side!

The secret of a good cartoon character is...

would it make a nice SOFT TOY?

2. Trace your traces

3.
And get

faster

every

time

you do

a trace,

and

simplify it!

SKILL – All the best cartoonists are extremely skilled in traditional drawing, and confident enough to know how to simplify and exaggerate (and when) for comic effect. Skill takes practice. Genius takes a bit more...SO KEEP PRACTISING.

TIP – Make it easy – find two features that make your character recognisable. Exaggerate them a bit...then see how small you can draw it – it's got to be really simple and have a distinctive outline! Draw it over and over – it'll settle down into a shape that you find easy to put into lots of situations...and it will develop its own personality! Have a conversation with it – it may surprise you!

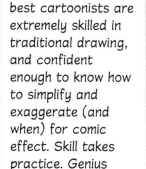

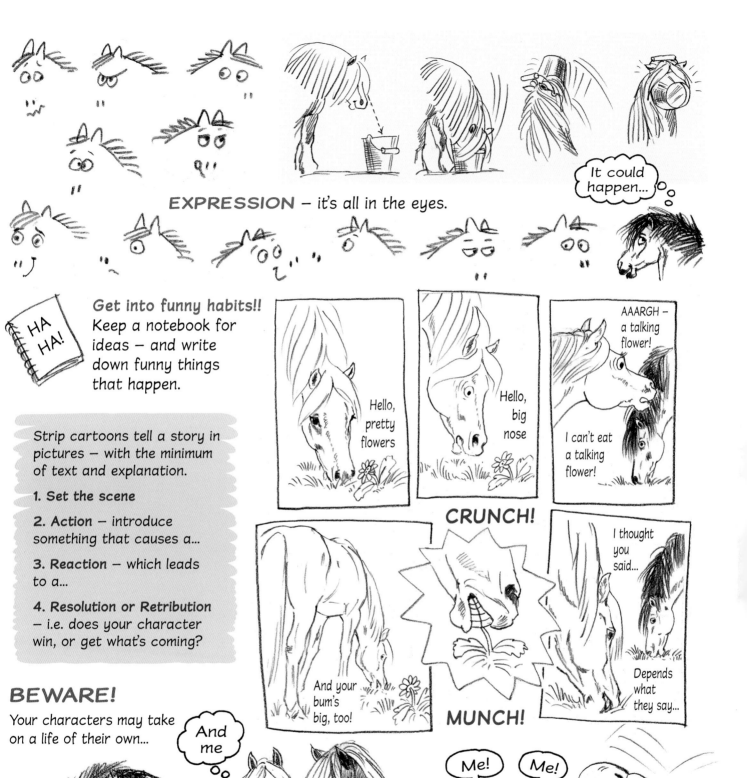

EXPRESSION – it's all in the eyes.

It could happen...

Get into funny habits!!
Keep a notebook for ideas – and write down funny things that happen.

HA HA!

Strip cartoons tell a story in pictures – with the minimum of text and explanation.

1. Set the scene

2. Action – introduce something that causes a...

3. Reaction – which leads to a...

4. Resolution or Retribution – i.e. does your character win, or get what's coming?

BEWARE!

Your characters may take on a life of their own...

Like me

And me

And me

Me! Me!

?**""""@*!!

Hello, pretty flowers

Hello, big nose

AAARGH – a talking flower!

I can't eat a talking flower!

CRUNCH!

And your bum's big, too!

MUNCH!

I thought you said...

Depends what they say...

45

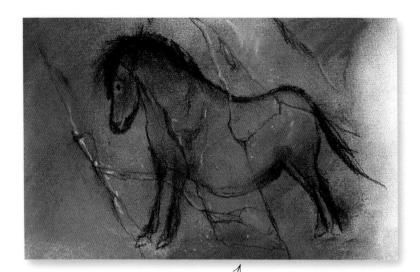

Ponies from the Past

From the dawn of civilisation...to the Renaissance...to modern times...in war and peace...in sport, and work and mythology.

Me as a cave pony

and Trevor as a Renaissance war-horse!

There's something wonderful about horses and ponies that has always inspired artists...**AND STILL DOES...**

After the invention of photography, artists could study *actual movement*, which has led to a revolution in equestrian art!

Rosie as an eighteenth-century racehorse galloping – idealised, long-legged, pointy nosed, but so-o-o elegant!

It was said that photography would kill off art HA! HA! HA! HA!

Rosie in stop-frame photoshoot at the gallop – see the difference – looking REAL and still lovely!

(Not Picasso at all)

(Not *quite* Stubbs)

(Only *a bit* like the illustrated Black Beauty – Lucy Kemp Welch.)

Is it Trevor or Rosie or me?

I can't tell either!

It's never too early to start to **THINK LIKE AN ARTIST!**

★ Take your drawing seriously.

★ Use your imagination.

★ Be teachable.

★ Challenge yourself, and don't ever be discouraged – learn from your mistakes.

Even top artists are always learning new things and trying out new techniques – AND YES! They make mistakes too!

SCRAP BOOK

Start a scrap book for useful pictures and horsy stuff – and articles about art – lots of different things for references... you never know what might come in useful!

Find a box for the photos you take – use them to give you original ideas for pictures for exhibitions and competitions.

AND

Keep sketchbooks for doodles and drawings, ideas for pictures, things to remember, and **IMPORTANT THOUGHTS!**

Read lots of books on horses and art.

Ooh! Did I do that?

Info Plus

Look up www.drawingponies.com for more news and views and photos of us; at home and out and about!

It's got more info and ideas about **drawing ponies**, AND features interviews with the best equestrian artists around, talking about how they got started, what they like doing, and their top tips!

AND there's a gallery for your best pictures – you can look at what other people are doing too! ...and lots more!

The Society of Equestrian Artists (SEA) has a fantastic website; www.equestrianartists.co.uk, where you can see a vast amount of work by serious contemporary artists (their members can be amateur or professional, established...or just starting out), a newsletter, and reviews and publicity for their exhibitions and workshops.

J.A. Allen, Specialist Equestrian Publishers, have a great website www.allenbooks.co.uk where you can browse their booklist and buy some really useful equestrian material direct from the publisher (including more copies of this book!).